New Journey, New You!

Guide to Spiritual Growth

CESCYIA STEVENSON

Cescyia Stevenson

New Journey, New You!

New Journey, New You!
Guide to Spiritual Growth
Cescyia Stevenson
ISBN: 9781736745595
Copyright ©2021 by Cescyia Stevenson
All rights reserved. No part of this book may be reproduced in any form whatsoever, including information storage and retrieval systems, without permission in writing from the author—exceptions by reviewers, who may quote brief passages in a book review.

Edited by Shawn Jackson
Cover by Design Place LLC
Published by One2Mpower Publishing LLC

Cescyia Stevenson

Acknowledgement

I truly thank God for using me as a vessel to help those who need to hear and read his word. I would like to thank my uncle Sean Robinson for allowing God to speak through him regarding me writing a book in the early 2000s. Very thankful for my friend LockMarie for encouraging me to actually write this book in 2018. To one of the pastoral team members from the Potter's House Dallas, thank for allowing God to speak through you about the publishing of my books.

Thank you to my sounding boards for this book- my aunt Cassandra Barrett and my sister friends Corretta D. and Evonne J., To Lady Wanda Kendrick thank you for your extended encouragement and prayers. To Apostle Louis and Prophetess Nitarsha Gordon thank you for pushing me towards purpose.

Cescyia Stevenson

Preface

As a college student, I went through several seasons where I was trying to do things the way I used to do them as a high school student. For example, in high school, I didn't have the resources at home to help me with some of my difficult homework assignments, so I would do what I could to figure it out and by trial and error. Yes, I would go to my teachers and ask for help, but it was more about me solving my own problems in my own way. This behavior was not healthy because in my first fall semester in college, I tried to use that same method, and I failed. One of the student counselors spoke with me and asked me what happened. After telling her my approach, she told me the most important words anyone could say to me at that time, "Resources were available to help, but because you did not ask for help, these are the consequences."

Outside of making my first failing grades as a college student, I had the burdens of people asking me how I was going to pay for school, academic counselors telling me I didn't deserve to be a student at the University of Florida, and people expecting the worse—I would fail and drop out and have multiple children. I came to college knowing people were expecting me to fail, open wounds that stemmed from rejection and low self-esteem. I had learned how to move forward through forgiveness, but I had not mastered being fully delivered from people's opinions about me. I went around campus participating with different organizations i.e., University Gospel Choir, Welcome Week Committee, Black History Month, and Step Show Committee, just to name a few, smiling on the outside, but I was truly hurting on the inside. I wanted to be able to participate in different groups and make good grades, but then I found myself facing an unsettling truth—I needed to learn how to love myself for who I was and understand it takes time for people to get to know you and understand how valuable you are. Things got a little hard for me dealing with the wounds I had, and it got to the point in my college life that I sought professional counseling because I could not fully comprehend the decisions I was making and why. It wasn't until I got into a relationship with Emilio, whom God told me no to, that the light bulb started to come on.

    I met Emilio at a party, and he seemed to be down-to-earth and very nice. His smile was very attractive, but that was all I knew. I went back and described him to a few friends, and they knew who he was and where he worked. Wanting to know more about him, I started pursuing to get to know him. God began to speak to me and show me through Emilio's actions that he was hiding something. Emilio asked me to use my car one time, and I was very uneasy about allowing him to. Although I had driven Emilio to his parent's house before, I still wasn't comfortable with allowing anyone to drive my car without me being present. This was a learned behavior from growing up that people will not treat your personal items like you would.

When God started showing me in my dreams Emilio with two kids, I began to scratch my head because I couldn't understand. One day, I was taking one of my friends somewhere on campus, and she mentioned she saw Emilio's mother at the hair salon. She went on to tell me Emilio's mom was bragging she had twin grandchildren on the way. My response to my friend was Wow! Emilio's secretive behavior and his asking me about having kids and a family came full circle. God was trying to tell me, but I wasn't listening. I had walked in disobedience for some months, and as a result, I had to deal with the consequences. My grades suffering, my self-esteem all over the place, and of course, all the other burdens I carried brought me to a place that I needed God more than ever.

    When I asked God to get me out of the situation I got myself in, he did just that! I began to pray and seek God more. I stopped gambling with my soul and truly recommitted myself to God. Emilio didn't know that I knew about his relationship and the children he was expecting. For me, this was the second guy I was involved with that God showed me the same dream, and it spoke to what was happening in both of their lives. I cut it off with Emilio and kept on moving. Because I had gone through four wisdom teeth being pulled, an inflamed arch that led to therapy, and then getting sick that caused me to medically withdraw from some of my classes, I knew cutting it off with Emilio was the best option. This spiritual detox came into existence when I recommitted myself to God. The process started off with me wanting to do the will of God after walking in disobedience of seeing Emilio when God said no for so long. The process came with me moving to where he needed me and even speaking what he needed me to speak. God has used this detox to peel the layers of lies, hurt, deceit, and poor decision-making. I learned how to let people go and most of all, I learned how to embrace and walk out the will of God for my life.

What Should You Expect from This Spiritual Detox?

This spiritual detox is truly for those who desire to have a spiritual transformation that leads to spiritual growth and prosperity. This is an individual process, but if you decide to do this detox with someone or a group of people, seek God to ensure it is something He wants you to do. The purpose of this spiritual detox is to allow God to shift your thinking and the way you make decisions to help you get to your destiny. Keep in mind, if you do the detox with someone or a group of people, everyone's path is not the same, and people's motives and intentions may change throughout any process. This detox is not an extreme challenge that will ask you to do something so farfetched you are not able to do it or complete it. Please note that everyone may not get the same results from this detox, but the common result should be that everyone draws closer to God through studying his word and allowing him to give clarity where it is needed.

Cescyia Stevenson

Introduction

When I took this challenge, I was in a position that I needed to hear from God. As we grow in Christ, sometimes we pick up habits and allow people to speak in our lives, but we never truly process what God is saying to us directly. I had to learn to ask God to allow me to receive what he needed me to receive from the sermons at church because I was soaking in everything but sometimes finding myself in a state of confusion. God wants us to live a life that is peaceful and not confusing.

People get tired of making the same old mistakes and following old spiritual rituals that they can't understand. People desire a change that will help them to become better people. In the Bible, the Israelites lived in slavery and wanted to be freed, but it didn't seem like it was ever going to happen. God raised up Moses to become their leader to help them become free. In Exodus 14, the Israelites are finally free from slavery, but they have a really hard time accepting it. The Israelites lack of acceptance of their freedom lead them to their own demise. Illustrated in Numbers 14 is God's response to the Israelites behavior regarding his provision and plans for them. The attitude of the Israelites shows how people act today towards God when they ask Him to heal, deliver, and set them free, but according to how they want it.

    Detoxing is a cleansing process that helps a person to remove anything that is toxic out of their system. This spiritual detox does the same, but it affects the spiritual aspect of a person's life. Before jumping into the exercises, here is an overview of what to expect in each phase.

1. The first exercise deals with knowing your purpose and getting the directions you need

from God for the season that you are in. There were times when I experienced anxiety and confusion because I could not identify my purpose and the direction God needed me to go in. When you know the purpose, then God's direction follows. As a part of knowing your purpose, you will be able to identify your role in other's life. Sometimes God will shift our purpose in the lives of the people we hang out with or even the people we date, jobs, activities, and ministries. A more in-depth explanation of this is made in the first exercise.

2. Decision and ministry are in the second exercise because they are an extension of the first exercise. When we know our purpose and the direction God is leading us, then we can move forward with making healthier decisions and walking into the ministry God has given us. One of

the hardest things for people who help others out a lot is to say no sometimes. We add more to our plate than we need to, and God must figuratively slap our hands a few times to tell us to leave certain situations alone. Sometimes we experience disappointments because we assumed the path we were taking was the one God was leading us down. At the end of the second exercise, you should be able to identify your ministry, and your decision-making should be more Christ-centered rather than self-centered.

3. The last exercise focuses on moving forward and embracing all God has poured into you during the first two exercises. This part of the exercise is positioned to help you to focus more on living and walking out the changes you have learned during the process. You should

be able to see the pre-detoxed person versus the spiritually detoxed person.

Preparation for the Detox

Using a notebook or journal to record the things God speaks to you is highly recommended. Writing down your responses to some of the questions may help you bring things into perspective. There have been numerous times I have looked back at my journal with notes from my detox, and I have been able to identify the root of common problems. Sometimes we deal with the same issue in different phases, so it pays to write down what God speaks to you because what he says maybe the key to unlock the next chapter in your life. It is important to go along with what God is speaking and guiding you to work on because he knows the assignment he has called for you to do in the future.

Cescyia Stevenson

The Process of Finding Purpose

As a college student, I laid across my bed in my apartment, and I asked God what is it that you want me to do. God clearly spoke to me that night about what my purpose was and what he wanted me to do. I could hear God clearly because I got to a place where there were no distractions and outside noises. God can speak to you while you are exercising on the treadmill or even running. Sometimes he will speak to us in our dreams. God spoke to me that night in my room, and I began to write what He was telling me. Since God had my attention, He knew I was in a place to receive instructions and walk them out. If God speaks to you through a dream, make sure you pray and ask Him for revelation. Don't try to figure out what the dream means because sometimes the dream isn't about you, but other people. Often God will reveal your purpose or direction through your dreams. Be careful who you share your dreams with because not everyone who hears the dream has your best interest. I shared a dream with someone, and I noticed the response from the individual. It appeared the individual may have been looking for answers concerning something he or she was experiencing, and my dream seemed like the answer. Later, I found out God was preparing me for a season that I was approaching, and the individual that was in my dream was a part of that season. If God is trying to help you get to your future, then the enemy will stop at nothing to get you off course. John 10:10 (NIV) says, "The thief comes only to steal and kill and destroy; I have come that they may have life, and have it to the full." This verse illustrates the enemy, known as Satan's, characteristics. If the enemy can get us distracted, then he has accomplished stealing our time, killing our vision, and destroying our hopes for a better future.

Often the soil (soil here is referring to our spiritual foundation) we are trying to plant spiritual things in is in bad shape due to a lack of nutrition and care. We should never get to the point that our spiritual soil lacks the nutrition it needs for us to grow. God knows what our spiritual soil needs, so he brings people into our lives that will help us to take care of our spiritual soil. God will send someone who will speak into our lives to cause correction or even encourage us to push into greater things. The next part of this section focuses on the exercise.

Exercise 1

Scriptures to meditate on:

Jeremiah 10:23 (NLV) I know Lord, that our lives are not our own. We are not able to plan our own course.

Psalm 32:8 (NKJV) I will instruct you and teach you in the way you should go; I will guide you with my eye.

Psalm 119:133 (ASV) Establish my footsteps in your word, and do not let any iniquity have dominion over me.

Starting Prayer:

God, help me to understand my purpose and the direction in which you are leading me. Help me God to receive your instruction with an open heart and mind. God help me to focus and take the necessary steps to be in your perfect will. In Jesus Name, Amen.

New Journey, New You!

Just like regular seasons change, so does our spiritual seasons change. God wants us to understand some of the things we have been doing or people we have been connected to can no longer handle where we are going. For example, God needed Abram to leave his family and go to a place where he would bless him (refer to Genesis 12). Abram obeyed God, but there was one issue—his nephew Lot, whom he loved. Abram allowed Lot to come with him on a journey God only called him to. Because God's promise was with Abram, God allowed confusion to fall between Abram and Lot's servants, and they parted ways. Abram understood God's purpose for his life was much greater than what he understood. There are some things we need to part ways with because God has specific blessings assigned just for us and our future generations.

God, what are the things that you need me to part ways with?

I was a part of a ministry and became active with different groups within the church. As I began to discern the people around me, I noticed many of them didn't know their purpose in life. It got to the point that I was agitated and was ready to throw in the towel. I didn't want to participate in some of the events that were happening because all I could see was the popular crowd always getting called upon to do things. Some of the individuals were nice at times, only to find out information about me or others. It got to the point that I questioned their love for Christ. The positive things that people were saying to me didn't matter because I was focused on what I thought was God's purpose for my life. I had a gentleman who told me how much he appreciated my ministry on Sunday morning and told me to keep it up. A Hollywood celebrity who attended the church even recognized who I was. Again, the compliments were nice, but I was seeking something more meaningful.

    When things got to the point that a change needed to happen, God moved me to a different city in another state to get me back on track to fully understanding my purpose. During Wednesday night Bible Study in the new city, God met me at the altar that night. I went up for prayer, and as the minister began to pray for me, the heaviness began to leave me. The Holy Spirit started working on my heart and mind. While driving home from that service, God continued to work on me. Once I got home, I began to write in my journal everything that happened in the previous city, and then God began to pour into me the truth I needed to acknowledge. I was truly set free that night. I no longer looked at what happened in the previous ministry as an issue but as a learning experience. I learned not everyone knows their purpose in life, and even when they do, some choose not to walk it out for whatever reason. That night I parted ways with the offenses I carried for too long.

Examine Yourself

It is important to start out by examining yourself. The Bible records that a man should look at the beam in one's own eye before looking at someone else (Matthew 7:3). Self-examination requires that you as an individual be honest with yourself regarding the things you have done versus the things you know you should be doing. The hardest part of life is acknowledging we have been traveling down the wrong road for a long time or the fact that we got distracted and never returned to doing what we were supposed to be doing. Life has a way of catching up with you. In one season of my life, I was walking down the right road, but I was distracted by others around me.

Journal Exercise—Write down the answers to the following questions.

1. Does God's purpose for this season match what you think your purpose is? How much different are they from each other? Jesus said, "Lord, not my will, but your will be done (Matthew 26:39,)," as it relates to walking in your purpose.
2. What is God speaking to you?

After answering those questions, take some time to read over your responses and allow God to expound on what he is trying to show you. It may take you a couple of days to soak in what God is speaking to you. Be open to what God has to say! Sometimes we reject what God says because it sounds much different than what we are used to. For example, in Exodus 3 (NIV), God speaks to Moses from a burning bush and tells him to go to Pharaoh to let his people go. In verse 14, God gives Moses further instructions to tell the Israelites, 'I am has sent me to you.'" You can imagine what Moses was thinking in his head. God's purpose for Moses was to use him as a vessel to set His people (Israelites) free. Your purpose may not make sense to you, but the people who need you will understand who you are in their life. The next part of this exercise focuses on our purpose in these areas: family, friends, and significant others.

Relationships

As humans, we want to help as many people as we can because we feel it is the Christ-like thing to do. Helping others makes us feel like we are making a difference in the world. Sometimes helping others can become a burden, especially when we get so consumed with trying to find a resolution to someone else's problems. God wants us to have healthy relationships that don't send us spiraling down. Knowing who God has connected you to helps you to move in the things God has intended for you to move in. Engaging in any new relationship should include God at the beginning.

As Christians, we should not be naïve regarding where people are spiritually. Most people will show you through their actions and conversation where they are spiritually. The term fake it to you make it can be used because some people fake where they are in Christ. In 1 John 4:1(ESV) says, "Beloved, do not believe every spirit, but test the spirits to see whether they are from God because many false prophets have gone out into the world." We must circle back to God because he knows those who are operating in His Spirit or not. For this area, make sure you understand the assignment God has given you for the people you are connected to. This will help you avoid toxic people that are sometimes camouflaging themselves. It will also help you avoid any unnecessary emotional, physical, or spiritual soul ties.

Your position and posture matter when it comes to hearing from God. One of the things I have either personally experienced or seen first-hand is the development of relationships from a healthy or toxic point-a-view. I have watched people get into relationships because other people boosted the relationship up based upon the outside appearance and what "looked good together." In those situations, I have seen so many people get hurt and God had to really restore both individuals. Getting into a relationship with someone is not just about a physical need, but for the purpose of God's kingdom. You may be single and have children. Every person that you date is not meant to be the next "mother" or even "father" to your child or children. Some people who God allows to influence your child or children's life are a part of his perfect plan. As we get older and reflect on the positive influences, we then began to understand why God allowed certain people to cross our path. God gives us free will, and according to Philippians 2:13 (ISV), "It is God who is producing in you both the desire and the ability to do what pleases him." No matter what your marital status: single, married, divorced, widowed, you should be able to identify if you have been chasing after God or a person.

Evaluate and Assess—Be honest about your relationships.

1. Do your friends push you forward, or do they allow you to go back to being who you were before you were saved?

2. When you interact with your friends, does your mind go into places it shouldn't, or do you feel you are disconnected? Your spirit man (intuition) will give you a clear warning of those who compromise your relationship with God.
3. Where does God fit in your endeavors? Does God really have full access and control of the direction you are going in?

In this next portion, let's address family and their purpose in your journey. As an individual, you will learn that family will be family no matter how life turns out for you. As children, we are often shielded from the truth about certain family members. When we get older, certain things about certain family members start to come out, whether it be a family member who seems to be kind but has an abusive nature (verbal or physical). God must always be our guide when we deal with family members with offenses. This simply means we have to be reconciled with the offense and allow God to heal the wound. It is a process, and it does not happen overnight. Sometimes God will separate you from your family to allow the healing to come forth. This does not mean you do not love your family, but this is a time God is bringing you to a place of being transformed and at peace.

The book of Ruth chapter 1 illustrates how Naomi goes through a couple of transitions that causes her to rethink her life. The first thing that happens to her is the death of her husband, Elimelech. Elimelech makes a life-changing decision to leave their country during a famine to head to another country that appears to be doing much better. One may think his decision was the right one considering he was looking out for his family; however, the country they were going to served idol gods. Elimelech's family survived other famines before where they were, but he was seeking to be in a place where he could live his life the way he wanted to. Elimelech's decision caused the course of his family's history to be changed. His sons did not heed Naomi's advice to return to their homeland, so they, like their father died.

As believers, we are quick to help our family members out, whether it is financially or even a listening ear. Sometimes we overextend ourselves in both areas because we do not pray and ask God how to deal with situations concerning our family members. We must be careful we are not crutches for our family members. Crutches are always rescuing others who refuse to take responsibility or control of their life. There are some learned behaviors from previous generations that exemplify a destructive path. Behaviors such as gambling, hustling others through promises that will not be kept, and mismanagement of money, to name a few. Because we know family members who are like this, we must use the wisdom that can only come from God to help us when we are helping our family members. There are seasons when God will allow you to help certain family members because he is transitioning them into something greater, but other than that, we should not always volunteer to help just because we feel sorry, but rather ask God what the best way will be to help family members.

Naomi tried to give her sons sound advice about handling their inheritance and making life decisions, but they had no interest. You may say that it is crazy to be constantly asking God when to help and not help a family member, but I have learned from experience that sometimes family members expect more than what they ask for. For example, you may have a family member who always talks about how bad other family members have treated them over the years (i.e. family members wouldn't help them when he or she was down and out or stopped talking to them because they were not able to pay them back in a timely manner) as a way to manipulate you to give them what he or she wants. Yes, it is manipulative and deceitful, but many people get away with it all the time. We can no longer ignore the signs of a toxic family member but rather take the time to deal with the issues at hand.

Journal Exercise—Write your answers in your journal.

1. What are some common financial behaviors you have observed from your family?
2. What types of financial behaviors do you exemplify? Do you like to save money or invest? Do you like to budget? Are your financial behaviors the same as your family's?

3. When it comes to your family, do their opinions strongly influence your decisions?
4. Have you ever found yourself in conflict between God and your family as it relates to the life changing decisions you have made? Who did you go with? What was the outcome?

The journal questions asked above are used to stimulate your mind to think about how you would handle a financial situation that Naomi lived through with her sons. Secondly, to open your eyes to see whether your family members have presented themselves financially as one thing but hearing them talk about their financial struggles tells you that participating in every retail sale is not financially healthy. In Matthew 25:14-30 the Parable of the Talents tells believers to be wise in what they do with the resources God gives to them. Out of the three servants, only one didn't understand the principle of sowing and reaping. He thought if he kept what his master gave to him, his master would benefit from having one investment that had no growth.

Reflection

I started this challenge when I was a sophomore or junior in college, and over the years, God has brought me back to this same process to help me move forward. In a recent season, I was challenged by two separate ministers about my purpose and the direction God was taking me. As the Holy Spirit began to speak to me through them, I knew I needed to get back on track because God was letting me know I needed to move forward. As I began the challenge in 2017, God began to deal with me in the areas listed above. When I faced another challenge within this challenge, God sent another minister to help be a "mid-wife" to push me to walk out what God was speaking to me. Because of the first exercise challenge, I was able to identify my purpose in other people's lives as well as identify the purpose of others, including family members, in the current season I am in. At the end of this challenge, I cut my hair off and rid myself of everything that was old attached to me. It felt good, and I had the peace that my spirit-man needed.

I learned I couldn't fix everyone's problems, nor did I need to take on other people's issues. Next, not everyone could walk with me in the direction God was taking me. I had to stop forcing people who I thought had good intentions to fit into God's will for my life. I found out through this first exercise I had people who would challenge what God spoke to me to do. It was through their conversation with me, I found out where they stood, and I was glad God exposed their intentions so I could cut off the relationship. God also helped me to identify learned behaviors that controlled how I responded to people. I had to take full responsibility for the things I allowed to happen. In becoming more intentional with everything I did, I started asking God more "what is your purpose for this connection."

Decisions/Ministry

This exercise looks further into purpose and direction as it relates to the decision an individual makes and how it affects his or her ministry. Sometimes we make decisions based upon our emotions or outside influences. When people make emotional decisions, it can cause many issues. Regret is one of the first issues people often deal with. The questions, "Why I did this? Why didn't I see this before it happened?" are among the many questions that are asked. Regret also leads to unforgiveness. Unforgiveness comes in with regret because the consequences of our actions remind us of how we possibly jumped into something without taking the necessary time to think it through. Not being able to forgive yourself can lead to depression and other issues. In addition to emotional decisions, outside influences can have the same effect.

Outside influences can be defined as friends, acquaintances, or even anyone who is willing to offer you advice. When people constantly give us advice about how we should do things but never direct us back to God, meaning never encouraging us to pray to God or seeking him, we should be concerned.

In making any decision in life, God will never encourage his children to make an emotional decision. As a matter of fact, God will always provide the necessary tools to help people walk in the path He has chosen for them to walk in. God's path is always straight, and His word will always guide us. Before reviewing this section, take the time to think about the major decisions you have made. Has pride and self-ambition been the driver of your decisions? *Meditate on this:* God help me to see where I am making or have made decisions based upon my emotions, logic (it just feels like the right thing to do), and from the advice of others (people giving their opinion about the situation).

Exercise 2

Scriptures to meditate on:

1 Kings 22:5 (CSB) But Jehoshaphat said to the king of Israel, "First, please ask what the Lord's will is."

Colossians 4:17 (NLT) And say to Archippus, "Be sure to carry out the ministry the Lord gave you."

Decisions come with the fine red print most people ignore. Philippians 2:13 (KJV), "For it is God which worketh in you both to will and to do of his good pleasure." God gives us free will and most people take full advantage of it, but people also forget, one shall reap what he or she sows (Galatians 6:7). God is merciful, and He does extend his grace to us all. The world has believers believing the answers they need lie within the world. Romans 12:2 (ESV) says, "Do not be conformed to this world, but be transformed by the renewal of your mind, that by testing you may discern what is the will of God, what is good and acceptable and perfect." Here are some common decisions people often make: What church to attend, Where should I work or live? Should I date or marry this person? First, let's address the church you decided to attend, then employment, and lastly, relationships.

Church

Jumping from church to church has become a profession for a lot of people. People move from church to church because they fall out with certain people and how they do things. People in this section can be both licensed ministers as well as the general church membership. Because more people are starting to research certain things that have been said in the church, more people are starting to move away from ministries that are teaching religion based upon what has been said as a result of past generations. Most importantly, people have jumped from one church to another church because they refuse to submit to the leader of the church and their hesitance to truly submit to the will of God. Submitting to God is not a controlling mechanism but promotes humility. In the book of 1 Peter 5:6 (KJV), it says, "Humble yourselves therefore under the mighty hand of God, that he may exalt you in due time". We often miss the answer to our prayers because we are so headstrong about what we know will "happen." Consider submission as a place of humility. It is important to ask yourself these questions and write a response in your journal.

1. Lord, what is the purpose in which you have called me to the church I am attending or leading?" Understand that

throughout the Old Testament, God assigned different people to lead his people for different purposes, i.e. the exit out of Egypt, the crossing over into the promise land.
2. Am I just attending church out of ritual or am I attending because God has purpose for me being there?

God intended for His children to be challenged to step out on faith in all areas of their lives. Stepping out in faith could mean for some people facing the issues they are running from and truly being reconciled. That may not seem like something of faith to you, but when someone has been walking in fear for a long time, it takes a lot for them to even get to the past the surface of the issue long enough to see God has already worked it out.

Over the years, I have learned the importance of being at the right church and under the right leadership. God has given every pastor a group of people to lead and cover. In general, a pastor should be able to speak into your life without knowing your name. This means your church ministry should be pushing you towards studying God's word more and drawing closer to Him. If you are not experiencing this, then maybe there is an issue. Through prayer and fasting, God can reveal to you what the issue is.

Be aware of church cults! These are ministries that attract people with good entertainment and soothing words that causes people to draw towards their ministry without questioning any of their practices. The book of 1 John 4:1 (ESV) says, "Dear friends, do not believe every spirit, but test the spirits to see whether they are from God because many false prophets have gone out into the world." There are ministries that label themselves as a Bible based church, however, they mix the Gospel of Jesus Christ with other religions. Within these churches, they get people to do things that goes against what the Bible says. If the church tells you not to pray or even denounce that Jesus ever existed… run! When a church group tells you that no one can question what the leader says, and makes the church's image more important than God... RUN! There are plenty Biblical resources available that can help you to understand what the scriptures mean. Note your pastor should not turn into your idol god. We should respect and say encouraging words to our pastors, but when we say, the pastor said to do this or that, but we haven't taken the time out to pray and ask the Lord should we do this or that… that becomes a problem.

Place of Employment

As my season began to end at a job, God began to prepare me for what was yet to come. When I lost my job, I was not upset or caught off guard because God had spoken to me, "Your time is up." God wants His people in strategic positions so he can use them to bring glory to His name. If you pray and ask God to become a better person at work and he starts working on you because he wants to promote you to a higher position, don't find yourself rejecting God's promotion. Always remember that God knows what is going to happen down the road and the promotion you reject today may not come your way again. Be prepared for change as God shifts your working environment. You will always need to know your purpose so you can be effective in your work ministry.

Questions to meditate on and journal:

1. How do you see yourself in your current job position? Are you stale, stagnant, or flourishing?
2. Lord is my job consuming me to the point that I am pushing your work off to the side. God help me to be in the

right place and right position to be a blessing to your people.

Remember, your job should never become so important that you neglect your relationship with God.

Ministry

A person can have several areas of ministry God gives to them. For example, a person can be an intercessor, and, at the same time, God can give them the office of an evangelist. Or a person can be a midwife that helps to push people into the places God would have them to be and at the same time, be a missionary that travels to different places. If God called you to minister to people through writing plays, being a make-up artist, caregiver, or even a mentor, let no one or anything stop you from your ministry. Everyone's ministry begins at home first. If you are a single parent, your first ministry is your child or children. If you are married, your spouse is your first ministry. If you are single or dating, your first ministry is yourself. The question to consider, how can you minister to other people when you can't first minister to yourself.

Something to consider, married people should never find themselves ministering more to people outside their homes than they do for their spouse or children- God holds you accountable. Dating people must remember you are not submitted one to another as married people are. This is how many dating people lose their identity; they neglect doing the things God has called them to do to please their boyfriend/girlfriend (refer to I Corinthians 7). Be intentional by praying and asking God about the person you are consider dating, it will help you to end the cycle of dating with no expected end. Give God your whole heart.

Exercise Prayer

God, I no longer want to make hasty decisions that cause me to have regrets. God help me to make healthy spirit-led decisions that will cause me to continue to walk in your purpose and perfect will for my life. Lord, I desire to fully operate in the ministry you have given to me with no regrets. Lord, I no longer want to overlook what you are directly speaking to me to do. Help me identify those whom you have called to labor with me and help me to move away from those who come as distractions to stop me from fully ministering to my full capacity. As you bring the people to help me with my ministry, help me not to reject them as the people rejected Samuel when he became old (1 Samuel 8). God, help me to disconnect from situations where decisions were not made based upon your will for my life. God uproot every negative seed sown and planted in me to cause me to make the wrong decisions or cause my ministry not to come forth. (Seeds can be defined as words, actions, or deeds done)

Reflection

Some of the decisions I made were God-led, and others were based upon "outside influences." I had a lot of regrets because I short-changed God in my decision-making. Instead of waiting for God to really answer my prayer, I jumped up and started doing what I thought was right. It caused confusion and ultimately, God had to get me back on track. In the ministry area, I was hiding my true identity because I was afraid of how people would receive me. It wasn't until recently that I decided it was time to take off the mask. I didn't realize how many people needed me to be who I was as God intended. People will appreciate your ministry more when you are who God called you to be.

Cescyia Stevenson

The Purpose in Moving Forward

Healing in life means that one must move forward and embrace everything that comes along with it. If you have invested time in reading this guide, then this section should be easy for you. Once you have trained yourself to do something, it becomes natural for you to do it. Philippians 3:13-14 tells us, "To forget those things that are behind and press towards the mark for the prize of the high calling of God in Christ Jesus." When you forget those things behind you, it is basically saying be reconciled with those whom you need to be reconciled with and move forward. The world has people believing they can't move forward after heartbreak or even a series of life-changing events. Even when Jesus died, the disciples had to move forward. In Genesis 32:24-30,

Jacob came to a point in his life after going back and forth with Laban; he needed a change. When Jacob wrestled with a man-like figure, it took a lot out of him because he was in the fight of his life. Although Jacob was prevailing, the man knocked his hip out of place. Jacob's name was changed to Israel after everything was over. God desires to awaken the fight in us to want His will even more.

    Transformation and the renewing of your mind is a key process to all believers, as stated in Romans 12:2. Just like a caterpillar which spins into a cocoon only to transform into a butterfly, we as believers must do the same thing. The more God reveals to us, the more we should want to live a transformed life. Things to consider in this last exercise: spiritual hearing and vision, how have your relationships with others changed from the beginning of this exercise, and your dependency on God?

Solomon's son Rehoboam faced a dilemma when he begins to reign as king after his father dies in 2 Chronicles chapter 10. Rehoboam must decide whether the people will continue to work under harsh labor laws or will he lighten the load. When he consulted the elders that labored with his father, they suggested he lighten the load, but his friends he grew up with advised him to keep the harsh labor laws. Rehoboam took the counsel of his friends, and it caused many issues. Your question may be what relevance this story has with moving forward. Because Rehoboam's father Solomon, was the wisest man who sought God's wisdom, it was expected of him to walk in the same statue. In Psalm 37:30 (ESV)says, "The mouth of the righteous utters wisdom, and his tongue speaks justice." In moving forward in a healthy way, one must lean towards good godly counsel. Rehoboam didn't realize the advice his friends gave him was not the change the people needed to see a brighter future.

In Acts 9, Saul goes through a transformation on the road to Damascus. God uses Ananias to help with the process. Ananias had heard of all the things Saul had done to believers, and he was very skeptical about helping him, but he still did what God asked of him out of obedience. When Saul gained his sight back, he was no longer Saul, but God called him Paul, and he became an ambassador for Christ. Ananias represents many Christians who move personal feelings aside for the kingdom of God to be advanced. Deuteronomy 30:6 (NIV), "The Lord your God will circumcise your hearts and the hearts of your descendants, so that you may love him with all your heart and with all your soul, and live." Paul's transformation proved God could transform someone's heart that was hardened to being softened.

Exercise 3

Scripture to meditate on:

Ephesians 4:22-24 (BSB), "Put off your former way of life; be renewed in the spirit of your minds; put on the new self-created to be like God in true righteousness and holiness."

Self-Examination Reflective Moment

Relationships

In moving forward, God wants us to have intentional relationships that will allow us to grow and be fruitful. Who are the people and places God has spoken to you to cut ties with? Remember, in moving forward, you do not want to agree with anyone or anything that would place you in a toxic place. When Jacob was dealing with Laban, he was dealing with a toxic situation. Samson in Judges chapter 16 desired to be with Delilah, and it cost him his life. Samson was blinded by Delilah's outer beauty to the point that he let down his guard, and it affected his decision-making. Samson was in a toxic relationship but couldn't see it. No one can tell you how to feel about someone, but make sure at this stage in the detox you are making healthy strides at moving forward. Remember, you have the power to change your atmosphere, and if you silence the warning signs, the consequences will seem unbearable when they come. It is important to understand that your relationship with God requires a lot of work and time, just like any other relationship. After completing this exercise, you should see some type of change with your relationship with God.

Spiritual Hearing

As you move forward, don't allow pride to stop you from hearing from God. I always ask God to clean out my spiritual ears. Many people are like Samuel in

1 Samuel chapter 2, who had to learn the voice of God. When God called Samuel, he thought it was Eli calling him in the middle of the night, but Eli told him it wasn't him calling, but God. As you are moving forward, remember listening to different voices can hinder you from hearing God when he speaks. It is okay to be encouraged by inspirational messages on social media outlets, but it is not okay to become dependent on those messages. Although the messages may touch you emotionally or inspire you in the moment, remember that we must read our Bibles and pray every day in order to be spiritually filled. If we are constantly looking to hear from God through people, then we have allowed those people to become our idol gods. Consider this, when we are anxious, we are willing to do anything to get the answers we need. For some believers, this has caused them to seek out other mediums i.e., Tarot card readers, palm

readers, and even calling the psychic hotline to obtain answers.

How do I know I am hearing from God? When God tells us to do something, it goes against the norm. For example, in Judges 7, Gideon started out with 22,000 soldiers, and God told him to decrease down to 300 to fight a battle. Gideon won this battle through his obedience. When I was returning to the University of Florida to complete my degree, God allowed me to hear a message at church prior to leaving that would help me to walk into a door he opened on my behalf. The message was about giving, and it was a non-pressuring message. I gave in an offering from my financial aid money at my college church, and within a couple of days of giving, I received an unexpected scholarship to cover the remaining of my expenses for the semester. I was in total shock because I wasn't expecting it, but again, I was in a place that I could hear from God. Are you in a place that you can hear God without distractions? Have you made a true commitment to block outside voices and hear from God? Can you identify how many times you have ignored the voice of God?

Spiritual Eyesight

In Matthew 13:13 (NKJV) Jesus explains, "…[B]ecause seeing they do not see, and hearing they do not hear, nor do they understand." Why aren't believers able to see the things God is trying to show them? Believers are not able to see because they are distracted by the cares of this world. With everything happening in our world, believers don't see that more and more their thoughts and actions are being dictated by the actions of the world. Here is a prayer I have prayed before:

God, take the scales off my spiritual eyes that I may see clearer as I walk out the things you have called me to do.

God, I will allow your spirit to show me your truth in everything I do. God, as I move forward, I will see things as you see them, and I will move as your spirit leads. God strengthen my discernment.

Entertainment is going to be entertainment, but as believers, we should be careful what we allow to enter through our eye gate. In the time we are living in, more and more writers and producers are pushing their own personal beliefs through the television shows they create. Think about phrases you use or even habits that you have picked up based on the influence of shows you watched. I am not saying to be paranoid but look at some of the decisions you have made from watching and listening to certain things. In moving forward, we have to take control of what we feed our minds. When I look at our young people and notice all the songs they listen to, I begin to see the destructive pattern that has been created.

Reflection

At one point in doing this exercise, I started cutting out a lot of things in my life. Some of the music I was listening to and television shows I watched. I personally noticed a significant change in my spiritual health. I started paying closer attention to the lyrics of certain songs I liked and noticed my view on relationships in general was negative. God had to work on my heart and as a result, I view relationships differently now.

We are at the end of this exercise and now you as an individual have to make a decision about how you are going to proceed with your life. You can say there were some good points in this book, but I do not feel I got what I was looking for out of it. That may be true; however, life is a process. When we read something, it's like putting food in our mouth and chewing it. Once you swallow the food, that's when the digestive process starts. The same goes for when we are trying to make changes in our lives. You will face moments when some of the content of this book will meet you where you are, and you will be able to take the necessary steps to evaluate the situation and move forward with corrective action. Allow God to do his work in you!

New Journey, New You!

About the Author

Cescyia Stevenson is a licensed evangelist who has traveled to several countries while working in the government sector. Throughout her life, she has made it her mission to be a light in a dark place. Cescyia earned her undergraduate degree from the University of Florida in Television and Film Production and two master's degrees: Business Executive Leadership and MBA from Liberty University. After working in the government sector for seven years, Cescyia started caring for her grandmother full-time in 2014 until she passed in 2018. After her grandmother's passing, Cescyia returned to the educational field and has been using her life experiences to help troubled youth to get back on track. It is Cescyia's mission to share the Gospel of Jesus Christ to as many people as she can through her writing and productions.

New Journey, New You!

www.ingramcontent.com/pod-product-compliance
Lightning Source LLC
Chambersburg PA
CBHW060217050426
42446CB00013B/3096